PRECAUTIONARY TALES FOR GRANDPARENTS

summersdale

PRECAUTIONARY TALES FOR GRANDPARENTS

Summersdale Publishers Ltd
46 West Street
Chichester
West Sussex
PO19 1RP
UK

www.summersdale.com

Printed and bound in Great Britain by
CPI Mackays, Chatham ME5 8TD

ISBN: 978-1-84024-707-7

PRECAUTIONARY TALES FOR GRANDPARENTS

Some of which may be Read to the Young
for their Moral Improvement

JAMES MUIRDEN

INSPIRED BY
HILAIRE BELLOC

I dedicate these verses
to the memory of my parents
RONALD and DOROTHY MUIRDEN

FOREWORD

I was about ten when I was given a copy of Hilaire Belloc's *Cautionary Verses*. Lines read and re-read at that age sink so deeply into the brain that they cannot be disturbed by the layers that memory deposits on top of them. They are there for life.

When I wrote my *Rhyming History of Britain* in 2003, I unwittingly adopted Belloc-type iambic tetrameters because their cheerful rhythm had been thumping in my head ever since childhood. By coincidence, this was exactly fifty years after he had died at the age of 83. So I began thinking about ways in which I could pay my respects by 're-visiting' some of his verses, and started accumulating a collection in which The Lion, Rebecca, Lord Lucky and others of their kind frolic once more in the twenty-first century. I have been adding to the collection ever since, and this book is the result.

It is ironic that the man whose verses have made so many generations laugh was rarely happy himself. He had French and English parents, chose England as his home, wrote in English, and was above all a Catholic in a Protestant country. As an outsider, he was well placed to comment on the morals and manners of the comfortable upper classes of his time. In our less confident age, one does not have to be so detached to find mismatches between what is and what ought to be, and with Belloc's Beasts, Children and Peers as my guide, I have found plenty of inspiration.

Belloc published seven collections of humorous verses between 1897 and 1932. These were collected together and published in 1940 under the omnibus title of *Cautionary Verses*, which contains (if I have added them up correctly) a total of 67 poetical subjects plus 'A Moral Alphabet'. I have taken the title and first line of a substantial selection of these, retaining them under Belloc's general classification of Beasts (The Natural World), Children (Role Models and Bad Examples), and Adults (Peers and Other People), together with A Modern Alphabet, which may be helpful to those of the older generation who feel increasingly behind these changing times.

I showed my first efforts to David Eccles, who has now decorated five of my rhyming books, and he very kindly offered to join forces on this speculative venture. My wife Helen has cheerfully put up with the ghost of Belloc in the house, and I am also most grateful to Jennifer Barclay, commissioning editor of Summersdale Publishers, for turning speculation into reality.

James Muirden

CONTENTS

PART 1

THE NATURAL WORLD

Verses about Beasts, most of which are
suitable for reading to Grandchildren.

THE LION

The Lion, the Lion, he dwells in the waste,
And oddly enough he dislikes being chased
By carloads of tourists, who seem unaware
That it isn't good manners for strangers to stare.

But the thing that the Lion finds really frustrating
Is being observed when he feels like mating.
So at such times be tactful, and look to one side:
For he may be a Beast, but he's still got his Pride.

The Lion's allowed to have more than one Wife,
Which can't always mean a harmonious life.
When things get too awkward, he climbs up a tree
To ponder the problems of Polygamy.

This means that the Lion, like all of his kind,
May have a surprising amount on his mind.
So ask his permission, before you impose –
Or you risk ending up with a Scratch on your Nose.

THE TIGER

The Tiger on the other hand, is kittenish and mild,
According to a friend who planned to find one in the Wild.
But the lack of any feedback on what happened when they met
Confirms my growing doubts about the Tiger as a Pet.

The Tiger is symmetrical, so William Blake suggested.
That's a statement needing courage to be positively tested!
The only time his Right and Left could ever be reversed
Is when he's wondering which bit of you to gobble first.

THE WHALE

The Whale that wanders round the Pole
Deserves a bit of peace.
He's paid a catastrophic toll
For synthesising Grease.

So, Child, though you'd get a thrill
Harpooning one of these,
Restrain your innate urge to Kill,
Unlike the Japanese.

THE POLAR BEAR

The Polar Bear is unaware
Of why the BBC
Keeps sending programme-makers there
To probe his privacy.

And Oil underneath the snow
(Which everyone relies on)
Means boreholes sunk, and pipes that go
Way over the horizon.

And what of Global Warming, pray?
If temperatures keep rising,
The polar cap will melt away!
It's therefore not surprising

To find the Bear in some despair.
The best thing he can do
Is ask a Human if he'd care
To put him in a Zoo?

THE DODO

The Dodo used to walk around.
Alas! He lives no more!
But, being Dead, he is renowned,
Which he was not before.

THE ELEPHANT

When people call this Beast to mind,

They wonder, I suppose,

How large a Hanky he must find

On which to blow his nose?

THE RHINOCEROS

Rhinoceros, your hide looks all undone.
You face extinction, if the rumour's true.
You're anti-social, and you weigh a ton.
I miss the Dodo more than I'll miss you.

THE PYTHON

A Python I should not advise.
If given one as a surprise,
Return it, and explain
That if your neighbours called for tea
And noticed where their Pet must be,
They might not come again.

THE PORCUPINE

What! Would you slap the Porcupine?
Don't strike him from the rear!
Observe how every sharpened spine
(Shown in the picture here)

Defends him from such sly attack
When he is off his guard.
His back is not the place to smack
If you would smack him hard.

No! Mock your victim (if you dare)
And slap him in the face!
But all the same, you'd better wear
A gauntlet, just in case.

THE VULTURE

The Vulture eats between his meals,
Though snacks are bad for you –
Or so say nationwide appeals,
Which means it must be true.

The Nation's greatly overweight
From all this tucking-in –
Though it is just as bad, they state,
To be extremely thin!

But when you try to cross, alone,
The Serengeti Plain,
And realise that the home you've known
You'll never know again,

And high up in the burning sky
You see the Vultures wheeling,
Reflect, as you prepare to die,
On whether this Appealing

Has hit the target on the head;
For it's a patent fact
That Vultures never *look* well-fed
Although we know they've snacked.

But bear in mind the miles they flew,
The hours they spent looking,
Before they hovered over you
And saw their dinner cooking!

So turn your final thoughts to that,
And you will realise
It isn't snacks that make us fat –
It's *Lack of Exercise*.

THE CHAMOIS

The Chamois inhabits
Swiss mountains, where rabbits
Have nothing to chew
(For they can't eat the View),
And birds cannot fly
(They're already too high);
So there's not much around
Where the Chamois is found
Except Men, who ascend
(With the help of a friend)
On the end of a rope
In the desperate hope
That once up there, they'll find
One or more of its Kind,
And if they're too far
They will stalk the Chamois
Till they get to a spot
That offers a shot
Which they hope they don't miss.
What's the point of all this?
The risks are appalling –

They might find themselves falling,
Or killed by the weather!
The answer is *Leather*.
So the Chamois takes care
That there's nobody there
When reclined on a Peak.
It's not Wimpish or Weak
(As it would be in Man)
To do all you can
When you venture outside

To *Save your own Hide*.

THE LLAMA

The Llama is a woolly sort of fleecy hairy goat,
With a cheerful disposition and an insulating coat,
Which he needs at his excessive Altitude.

He's a native of the Andes (they're below us, to the left),
And a family that lost him would be utterly bereft,
For the Llama's many benefits include...

They can turn him into rugs, made from his shaggy outer hair;
They can use his woolly inner fleece for thermal underwear;
They can Burden him; and (lastly) he is Food.

There's a Kent or Sussex Llama, which is similar in kind,
Though the British Llama Farmer's Llama's vastly more refined;
But I fear that, like his cousins, he is woefully inclined
To use Precision Spitting when he thinks he's been maligned –
Which is, as you're aware, extremely rude.

THE VIRUS

The Virus is so very small
You cannot tell he's there at all,
Until his playfulness is seen
Displayed on your computer screen.
His puckish face is wreathed in smiles
As he corrupts your precious files;
And few things give him greater glee
Than wiping out your Memory
And leaving nothing, at a stroke
(Your backups, too, go up in smoke).
The best protection is, I think,
Not Firewalls but Pen and Ink.

PART 2

ROLE MODELS AND
BAD EXAMPLES

Grandparents should consider carefully the
suitability of some of these Verses before
reading them to younger Grandchildren.

ABOUT JOHN

Who lost at conkers, and earned his father some useful publicity

John Vavasseur de Quentin Jones
Had this world's values in his bones,
And knew the censure and disgrace
Of being pushed to second place.
He's now a top Financier
On twenty million pounds a year;
But in his pre-pubescent days,
When passing through the Conker Phase,
A shattering humiliation
Led rapidly to legislation
Outlawing this divisive game,
Which, to our everlasting shame,
Had been permitted to be played
Wherever Chestnuts cast their shade.

★

Where young John dwelt, in leafy Farnham,
An *Aesculus hippocastanum*
Grew by a place with swings and slides
And lots of other things besides,
Where children and au pairs could pass

A happy hour on the grass.
Yet no one had the sense to see
The sly corruption of this tree!
Those buds that held their secrets tight!
Coquettish chandeliers of white!
Then, with the first autumnal nip
Green spiky purses would unzip,
Disgorging from their pulpy lining
Forbidden fruit, so smooth and shining!
Do you recall that shameful thrill
When you would fondle one, and drill
A hole through which to pass a string,
And wind it up, and take a swing
At its opponent, shrunk and black,
And after an almighty *Thwack!*
Your chaste nut was no longer there,
Apart from fragments in your hair?

★

John Vavasseur de Quentin found
A splendid Conker on the ground
And having got it bored and strung,
He cried a challenge, aimed, and swung.
His certainty of being First
Was shattered when the Conker burst;
He punched the victor, stamped and bawled,
Ignored the au pair when she called,
And was Impossible at Tea.
His Father, an astute MP,
Drafted a well-reported speech

33

Praising the virtues of the Beech,
Whose nuts are not the tempting sort
That prompt such anti-social sport
(When losing causes such distress).
His campaign was a great success.
They took the Devious Tree away,
And children now may safely play.

ALGERNON

Who exceeded the speed limit, and paid the penalty

Young Algernon, the Doctor's Son,
Insisted on his daily run
Enjoyed a 100-mile hike,
Scaled mountains on his mountain bike,
Trained using weights five times a week,
Took stimulants for his physique,
Scampered on treadmills fast enough
To measure his amount of puff,
And borrowed (from his Father's store)
A gadget that he always wore
To tell him if his heart was beating.
His earthly tenure, though, was fleeting...
One morning, as he jogged to school
(He never walked – it was a rule)
He saw a masked man with a bag
Bearing the helpful letters 'SWAG'
Dash from a bank, pursued by yells
That added to the decibels
Of electronic howls and hoots.
Cashiers clad in trouser suits,
And male bankers wearing ties
(Who had the know-how to advise

On which Account would suit you best),
Plus others much less neatly dressed,
As customers so often are,
All madly shouting 'Stop that car!'
Poured out onto the pavement, where
A vehicle (no longer there)
Had waited for the thief to board.
Our hero, of his own accord,
Paused only to re-tie each lace,
Gulped oxygen, and then gave chase.
Along the High Street roared his quarry,
Causing a waste-disposal lorry
To knock an AA kiosk flat
And make a mess of Habitat;
It reached the bypass, skidding madly
(The driver drove extremely badly),
Then hurtled down the outer lane,
Sounding its horn. But all in vain!
Young Algernon was not out-run
However fast the wheels spun;
In fact, thanks to intensive training,
He was inexorably *gaining* –
At 90-miles-plus per hour
He still possessed reserves of power!
His shoes had worn completely through
(The upper parts had come in two);
His legs were just a blur; and then
He *overtook* the desperate men,
Forcing the speeding car to stop.
Thus the despairing Traffic Cop
(His blue lights flashing in pursuit)

Caught them red-handed with the loot
And booked them for excessive haste –
A charge our hero would have faced
Had not his Father's gadget said
That Algernon, his Son, was dead.

★

The church was filled to overflowing
To mourn his premature going
(Though sermon, sentiment and song
Did make the service rather long).
It was conducted by a priest
Who frankly labelled the Deceased
As 'something of a fitness freak',
And, warming up, went on to speak
Of how we shouldn't try to do
What we were not intended to!
Had we been meant to Ape the Cheetah
By being just as fleet, or fleeter,
We should possess four legs at least
To match this Supersonic Beast,
And possibly a couple more
(Although this arithmetic law
Breaks down, he could not but concede,
For life-forms like the millipede).
Let us (he said) be what we are,
Not emulate the Motor Car –
The motto for the Poor and Lowly
(That's you and me) is *Hasten Slowly*.

AUNT JANE

'Mamma,' said Amanda, 'I want to know what
Conceivable use it will be
To continue my studies until I have got
A second-class Honours Degree?

'This widely imposed educational goal
Is simply a plan for reducing
The number of people signed up for the dole
Who haven't a hope of Producing.

'A degree in your day, dear Mamma, was perceived
As a way to sift, sort and collate us;
But now every bog-standard Poly's received
Its own University status!

'It may hurt you, I fear, but I think it is right
To consider the whole situation.
I am not, let's be honest, excessively bright,
Nor do I foresee a Vocation.

'What talents I have I shall use to the full,
So let me be utterly frank:
If Father exerts his executive pull
To get me a job at the Bank;

'And you buy me a flat, and perhaps a small car,
I shan't trouble you ever again.
For I'll do what you did, my darling Mamma,
And start finding out about Men.

'Oh come on, Mamma – I know all about that!
You got through five Lovers at least!
That magnate who bought you a Bayswater flat;
Then two Judges, a Peer *and* a Priest...

'Tell Father? Come off it! The poor dear would be
Reduced to a state of distraction;
Provided, of course, I can drop the Degree,
And follow my own course of action?

'Oh thank you, Mamma! No, I shan't say *a word*.
I can't tell you who told me, of course.
But the fact that you haven't denied what occurred
Proves I had an impeccable source!'

CHARLES AUGUSTUS FORTESCUE

Who offered his seat to a lady, and abandoned a promising career in the Church

The nicest child I ever knew
Was Charles Augustus Fortescue.
Once he had learned to read and write
He took unparalleled delight
In sending letters on the dot
Acknowledging each gift he got,
And gave his seat, without a fuss,
To Ladies in an omnibus.
His parents chose a public school
Where decent manners were the rule
To waylay that hormonal stage
(Once quaintly called the Awkward Age)
When Charles might take to lager-louting,
Attacking panes of glass, or shouting
In terms no citizen should utter
While urinating in the gutter.
But these precautions were absurd!
He gloried in the Given Word
(In Greek, which scholars much prefer)
Including the Apocrypha,

Which made it clear, without a doubt,
That Ministry had marked him out.
The last exam for his degree
(Vocational Theology)
Saw him entrain at Chiswick Park
Quite certain of the highest mark
When in the vaulted hall he'd sit
And do his stuff on Holy Writ
Or options equally Divine.
This journey on the District Line
Was just the chance the Serpent sought!
The train filled up at Barons Court,
And Charles was quickly on his feet
To let a Lady have his seat,
But she refused the proffered place
And slapped him hard across the face
For daring even to suggest
She couldn't stand up like the rest.
The passengers were polarised:
Men thought his gesture ill-advised,
The women blamed the Fair Deceiver,
And someone pulled the little lever
That brought Discussion to a halt.
Charles argued that his only fault
Was having been brought up too well;
But all this took so long to tell
That when he reached his destination
They'd finished the examination.
He now rents an impressive suite
Near Selfridge's in Oxford Street,
Where he will outline (at a price)
The risks incurred in Being Nice.

41

FRANKLIN HYDE

Who argued that art is above life

His Uncle came on Franklin Hyde
Reading a Work he'd found –
Shelley's *Prometheus Untied*
(To be precise, *Unbound*).

> A gentleman of settled views,
> He said: 'I do not wish
> To see my sister's son peruse
> This play by Percy Bysshe!

'He's no role model for a Child –
That slave to Opiates!
Byron, and others no less wild,
Were his associates!

> 'His wife jumped in the Serpentine –
> His first, for he had two.
> The second one wrote *Frankenstein*,
> Which Ladies shouldn't do.

'*What?* Judge all Artists by their Art?
Their life's their own affair?
Take William Wordsworth, for a start!
No dirty linen there!

'You dare suggest that he could err?
He liked his Bit of Stuff?
A mistress, and a child by her?
Now that is quite enough!

'His sister's diary says *what?*
That she adored him too?
The apple cores he left to rot
She'd gather up and chew?

'And in her chilly bed she lay
In morbid ecstasy,
Wearing the Ring, before the day
He took his bride? I see...

'Well, maybe Percy Bysshe *does* need
A measure of restoring.
All right then, carry on and read –
But it's extremely boring!'

GEORGE

Who proved that profit is not necessarily incompatible with ethics

When George's Grandmamma was told
That she was getting far too old,
And her defunction and cremation
Would be a cause for celebration,
She moved forthwith to Benidorm
(Where decent manners are the norm),
Cut off her miserable heirs,
And gave her Marks & Spencer shares
To fund a novel Oxford Seat
In Ethics, which would help to meet
The need to have our Faith renewed
And challenge Moral Lassitude.

★

This outburst of hostility
Occurred when George was only three,
But was undoubtedly the force
That set him on his destined course;
For by the time he'd reached eighteen
This visionary youth had seen
The need to visit her in Spain,

Submerge their difference, and explain
That in his view she'd been quite right
To leave her wealth to help the fight
Against the moral degradation
Polluting our unhappy nation!
To take the Ethical Degree
(He said) was his priority –
But since his parents wouldn't pay,
He thought he'd hitch-hike all this way
And spend his summer serving Beer
(To pay for his initial year)
To those recusants most in need
Of a reconstituted Creed!

★

This spiel, as you may have guessed,
Left Grandma mightily impressed.
How could her uncouth son engender
A child so sensitive and tender,
Who was committed to beginning
A life of Moral Underpinning?
So, in an access of remorse,
She got him on the Oxford course,
With lodgings, and a little car,
And credit in the college bar,
Where, having so much common sense,
He'd be a healthy influence.
George, who had hoped to get (with luck)
Five hundred quid, was thunderstruck,
But thought he might as well appear,

And see if he could last a year.
It didn't take him long to find
How Oxford could direct the mind –
How he had nearly missed the turning
That pointed to prodigious earning!
The thesis for his Ph.D.,
Called *Profit and Morality*
(Greatly abridged for publication)
Became an overnight sensation.
Re-titled *Thinking Good Can Pay*
For markets in the USA,
It was a text that firms would give
To every young executive;
And, desperate to keep him there,
His College gave him Grandma's Chair,
Which pleased her so much when she heard,
Her heart burst, and she was interred.
George (as her only legatee)
Was left her villa by the sea,
Where Mum and Dad enjoy the sun:
So justice, in the end, was done,
With profits vastly in excess
Of what they'd be from M&S.

GODOLPHIN HORNE

Godolphin Horne was Nobly Born;
But having searched his soul, was torn
By conscience. Why should he possess
So much, and others so much less?
Why should a mere genetic fluke
Make this a Dustman, this a Duke?
His mental torment grew so great
He tried to give his whole estate
(In all, some thirty thousand acres)
To those unworldly folk the Quakers,
Who met in silence, and agreed
That it was not a Christian deed
To shoot the pheasants that were bred
In order to be filled with lead
By Foreigners, who paid the lord
Far more than others could afford
To cover things like mending fences
And miscellaneous expenses.
His offer having been dismissed,
Godolphin turned philanthropist,
And formed his land into a Trust,
By whose terms the Deprived were bussed
From urban Squalor and Decay
To spend a week or two away
In Nature's bosom, and to share
Large quantities of Scottish Air
In landscapes threatening and strange,

Where mobiles were out of range.
Since most of them did not survive –
Mortality was four in five –
The benefits were clearly seen
By Social Workers, who were keen
To lose their more demanding cases
In Highland bogs and suchlike places;
But, being told of their demise,
Tears welled into Godolphin's eyes.
'My friends, the facts are plain to see!
We cannot fight Heredity!
Some find a sermon in a stone;
Some cannot bear to be alone;
Thus we are born; and I'm afraid
We cannot change how we are made!'
These views did not exactly chime
With leading thinking of the time;
But having come to the conclusion
That Equal Rights are a delusion,
Godolphin was to wealth resigned.
The Trust's activities declined;
He planted yet more fir and spruce;
And on the land that is no use
For anything, he set up lots
Of wind-farms, selling gigawatts.
He's used the money so far raised
To have his Castle double-glazed,
And muses, in his study chair,
On why the World is so unfair.

HENRY KING

Whose chief defect was being
good at everything

The Chief Defect of Henry King
Was being Good at Everything.

HILDEBRAND

Who was frightened by a passing train, and received a useful lesson in relative velocity

'Oh, Murder! What was that, Papa?'
'That, Hildebrand, was Eurostar,
No sooner seen than gone!
Our own train's forty minutes late,
So let us sit and contemplate
This new phenomenon.

'The *Etoile* left at half-past two
From Platform 1 at Waterloo*,
And having flashed across your view
Will very soon be passing through
The Tunnel. Its *vitesse*
Alarmed you – but once over there,
The frictionless *Chemin de Fer*
Will speed it up enough to scare
Much braver hearts, my son and heir,
Than that which you possess!

'Across the plain of Normandy
The Eurostar's velocity,
Now multiplied by two or three,
Means that the onlooker will see
A brief transparent blur
(Or so, I'm told, it will appear
To anybody standing near).
Be reassured! You need not fear
Such apparitions over here!
No, no! We much prefer

> 'To *Hasten Slowly*. That's the way
> To get the most from every day,
> As we are doing now!
> What's that? Our train's delayed *again*?
> Oh well, we should be home by ten –
> Or midnight, anyhow!'

*   Since this poem was written, the high-speed St Pancras line has
    been opened, and Hildebrand would be even more terrified.

JACK AND HIS PONY, TOM

Who failed to take sensible precautions, and was killed

Jack had a little pony – Tom.

One day, while going like a bomb,

Tom pulled up short, but Jack did not,

And landed on this very spot

Where he has now been laid to rest.

So pause and inwardly digest

These chiselled words you're looking at –

If you go riding, wear a Hat.

JIM

Who proved that heredity, not environment, has the last word

There was a Boy whose name was Jim:
His Single Parent worshipped him,
Because he came to represent
Her ultimate experiment.
A student of the earnest kind
With higher matters on her mind
Than boisterous frivolity,
She stayed on for a Ph.D.,
And then, pursuing Fancy's flight
(And penniless), began to write.
Her gifts were spotted very soon
By somebody at Mills & Boon,
But she'd do better, so they said,
With less of Love and more of Bed.
And so, still in her research mood,
She sought verisimilitude
By sampling what she had missed
(For being amorously kissed
Was not a fate she had endured);
And soon her reticence was cured
By working for a drunken wreck
Who ran a pub in Tooting Bec.

This satisfied her research aims;
Its by-product was little James,
 (Not her original intention)
Who gave her art a new dimension;
And since it did her sales no harm
To have him pictured on her arm,
She joined the Literary Set.
Jim quickly learned the alphabet,
And having reached the age of three
He memorised the *Odyssey*,
Which presaged, it seemed fairly clear,
An intellectual career.
But Nature cannot be suppressed:
His father's genes refused to rest,
And soon the painful choice was made –
Jim opted for the Licensed Trade.
For Mum, this was a fearful knock;
But she has overcome the shock,
And writes her thousand words a day
On free supplies of Chardonnay.

FINE ALES
Ye Olde
Re-assertive
Gene
WINES & SPIRITS

MARIA

Who pulled a horrifying face, and brought her parents a considerable fortune

Maria loved to pull a face,
Especially in a public place,
When passers-by would shriek with fear,
Beholding such a ghastly leer.
Afraid that someone might report her,
The mother of this tiresome Daughter
Discouraged her, when it occurred,
By using a corrective word
Or two, though outwardly serene,
Befitting one who voted Green
(To help revivify the Air
They walked or cycled everywhere.)
But that's sufficient *mise en scène*.
Picture a Supermarket, when
There was a frank exchange of views
On why her mother should refuse
To buy her an unhealthy snack.
Maria having answered back,
Her mother was a trifle short,
Which made the angry girl resort
To grimacing; nor would she stop
Till horror spread throughout the shop.

Her mother, hearing the dismay,
Let fall a tin of cassoulet,
On which an innocent Trainee
Stepped, swayed, and lost stability,
Hitting, with devastating force,
A trolley-load of HP Sauce,
The transferred impetus propelling
The stuff towards the counter selling
Corned Beef and Spam, and other lures
To titillate the epicures,
(And where they baked their nice baguettes,
And little loaves you bought in sets).
In the confusion, someone's arm
Set off the General Alarm;
And since the baking oven was wrecked,
A safety circuit to detect
A fire risk, turned on the spray,
Concluding business for the day –
And nobody was asked to pay.

★

Their neighbour Abigail had been
A witness of this stirring scene,
And felt convinced that what took place
Was triggered by their Daughter's face,
Which, picked up by CCTV,
Could drag the wretched family
Into a hopeless situation
If they were pressed for compensation.
A law firm in the Shopping Centre

Invited anxious folk to enter
And have a consultation free:
YOU CANNOT LOSE: NO WIN, NO FEE!
Maria's mother went along
And told the Lawyer what was wrong.
'What? *Sue a customer*? No fear!
Don't go! You've got a goldmine here!
That tin... Too large for you to grip?
What? Some *commotion* made it slip?
I didn't hear that! Make them pay
For bad design – say 40 k.
Now then... It fell upon your toe?
Toes have gone up in price, you know!
What? Didn't hurt? I bet it did!
You *cycle*? Half a million quid!
Now, when you heard those shoppers shriek
(Your daughter, yes) you felt quite weak...
So noise upsets you? Always been
A nervous type? Since when? Fourteen?
They bullied you at school, I bet!
That's why you're easily upset!
What? Never bullied? Best of friends?
That's what your subconscious pretends!
You'll get a million, maybe two,
And we won't even need to sue –
A good Psychiatrist's Report
Should make them settle out of court!
Oh well, I think that's about all:
It sounds a reasonable haul.
What's that? You toss and turn in bed
Because the manager had said

That since the checkouts were affected
He'd let you keep what you'd selected?
That's *excellent!* We'll make them pay
For Mental Trauma – 50 k!'

★

Although Maria's mother knew
That this was what she ought to do,
She wondered if the compensation
Did not exceed the provocation.
But Money's strident voice out-shouts
Shy Reasonableness's doubts,
And with the booty, they acquired
A mansion many had desired,
Plus thirty acres, maybe more,
Which predicates a 4x4
(Or rather two), and they do not
Go out on bicycles a lot.
Maria's at a private school
Where Shocked Expressions are the rule;
And with the freedom money brings,
Which complicates so many things,
Her mother may soon need to find
Another helpful Legal Mind.

MATILDA

Who was too truthful to be successful in business

Matilda told such Dreadful Lies,
It wasn't such a great surprise
When she achieved a Ph.D.
In Corporate Identity.

But even though she Lied and Lied,
Her clients were dissatisfied.
Their images were still in doubt:
Too many facts were coming out!

She re-wrote everything she knew,
And made sure not a word was true,
Until at last she understood –
For this world she was much too good.

PETER GOOLE

Who paid too much attention
to the virtual world

Young Peter Goole, a child of nine,
Spent all his waking hours online,
Or playing games he would download
When others ceased to be *la mode*.
One day, his parents were persuaded
To let him travel quite unaided
(To give the lad an extra thrill)
By Underground from Dollis Hill
To Finchley Road, where he would meet
His Auntie, for a special treat.
But since, till then, he'd never tried
To focus on the world outside,
The station signs appeared so blurred
He couldn't read a single word,
And so, not knowing what to do,
He ended up at Waterloo.

The upshot of this sorry mess
Is not too difficult to guess –
His eyes were tested (left and right),
To gauge the defects in his sight.
The Ophthalmologist's report
Was clear, and admirably short:

'The rays from the computer screen
Have turned his retina bright green,
And in addition I have found
His eyeballs are no longer round.
To remedy this serious state
He must be forced to concentrate
On objects such as Distant Peaks.
Come back and see me in four weeks.
(Forgive me if I also mention
My Fee, for your esteemed attention.)'

The Boy, with glasses on his nose,
Was perched above the Alpine snows,
Where not a thing that he could see
Was nearer than Infinity.
This Real world he now espied
Left Peter feeling petrified –
The heights, the depths, the sense of space,
The utter *silence* of the place!
He flung away his specs, distraught,
And found the path down (as he thought);
But since he could not see his way,
He fell. His parents had to pay
An utterly colossal bill
To bring his corpse to Dollis Hill,
Where, as they laid him in the hole,
The Virtual world reclaimed his soul.

REBECCA

Who showed excessive initiative at an early age, and was restrained

A Trick that everyone abhors
Is circumventing prudent laws
That very reasonably give
A check on gross Initiative.
Rebecca's case will serve my need...
She was a headstrong girl indeed,
With no great appetite for school,
Which was not (in her argot) Cool:
The groves of learning did not hear
Her timid footfalls drawing near
The verdant Academic Spring.
Three teachers left for counselling,
A fourth contracted some disease,
The Head moved to the Hebrides;
But then a most persuasive ad
Pictured the pleasure to be had
If she could make her parents pay
For an Adventure Holiday.
This stimulated a discussion
That ended with a loud concussion
And left Rebecca in no doubt
That they would not be forking out;

But this refusal was the start
Of mighty efforts on her part.
She'd rise from bed at half-past four
To help the newsagent next door
Sort out the morning paper round;
Till seven-thirty she'd be found
A servant to the milkman's cart;
A bag of crisps, and she would start
Her school day, whence she'd hurry back,
Collect the papers in their sack,
Deliver them, and end the day
By washing up in Sid's Café.
This workload, as you might expect,
Had a significant effect
Upon her attitude in class.
Whole lessons, mornings, days would pass
In study so profound and deep
It outwardly resembled sleep;
The eager group that she had led
Lacked unity without its head,
Eschewing riot and commotion
For almost scholarly devotion.
The OFSTED team observed with favour
The vast improvement in behaviour,
Yet *not one teacher* showed concern
At this extraordinary turn,
Or worried what might lie behind
Rebecca's sudden change of mind!
But civic consciousness prevailed
Where *in loco parentis* failed.
Noting the hours that she kept,

Which manifestly overstepped
The legally encoded view
Of what a twelve-year-old should do,
A neighbour sent in a report
That cut Rebecca's efforts short.
Her sleeping hours re-imposed,
The girl no longer dreamed or dozed
When she reached school, but Did Her Bit,
And so another teacher quit.
A Child Psychologist suspected
That she was merely disaffected,
And so they had her sent away
On an Adventure Holiday,
Since when I hear that she's begun
To try to earn another one.

TOM AND HIS PONY, JACK

Whose father shot him through lack of practice

Tom had a little pony, Jack:
It sent him flying off his back
As Jack's had done, you will recall.
Tom wasn't really hurt at all
(The recommended headgear meant
That it, not he, received a dent),
But nonetheless he shouted 'Oh!'
His father heard him doing so,
And loaded up a Smith & Wesson
To teach the Frisky Beast a lesson,
But, lacking practice with the gun,
He missed the Horse and shot his Son.
So riding is, as you can see,
A dangerous activity.

PART 3

PEERS AND OTHER PEOPLE

These Verses are not suitable for reading
to Grandchildren of any age.

LORD ABBOTT

Lord Abbott's coronet was far too small,
But its dimensions mattered not at all
When lawyers for a distant cousin pleaded
With great success, that *he* should have succeeded.
Abbott was urged to fight this rude Pretender,
And should have been his family's defender;
But feeling harassed by their endless nagging,
He quickly felt his resolution sagging,
And let the arriviste enjoy the lot –
House, grounds, estate, the game birds to be shot
(Including all the necessary Beaters),
And fishing rights (10 k per hundred metres).
Rebuked by his astonished wife and heirs,
He left them free to wind up his affairs,
And decamped to a waste of stony earth
In Sutherland, of negligible worth,
Where nothing grew but lichen, heath and heather.
He built a simple hut against the weather,
And kept himself at all-but-zero cost,
Thinking, like Pericles, the world well lost.
He cleared some stones and scraped the soil bare,
And set to work to grow his daily fare –
He thought, as William Morris had opined, *
That honest labour fortifies the mind.
Before machines usurped the human fist
(Greatly enriching the Agronomist)
A village's entire population

LABOR VINCIT OMNIA

Ploughed, sowed and reaped, and practised crop rotation;
And now you had one fellow in a tractor!
This was, he thought, perhaps the greatest factor
That caused our present moral lassitude –
People no longer had to grow their food.
This was a view he'd openly propounded
Before his coronet had been impounded,
Although he'd thought it safer not to say
(When talking to John Humphrys on *Today*)
That outdoor labour with a fork and spade
Would be a far more beneficial trade
For many students getting A's and B's
Now studying for Futile Degrees.
But this had been his far from private thought
Late at his table, circulating port.

★

So, by his hovel made of daub and wattle,
Consuming Johnnie Walker from the bottle,
Beyond the range of any mobile mast,
The quondam Earl did honest work at last.
The polecat, stoat and weasel were his neighbours,
And often he would straighten from his labours
And take a little nip, and rest his eyes
Upon the products of his enterprise,
And sniff the rabbit stewing for his meal.
What spiritual ecstasy he'd feel!
Alas, like Pericles, he too had found
Unwanted nuggets lying on the ground,
For having left behind the world of greed,

Gold was the stuff of which he had no need!
But rumours of this disillusioned Peer
Gave somebody a dazzling idea –
A documentary for Channel 4!
One day, while he was sluicing in the raw,
A helicopter started to descend
And his sweet idyll clattered to an end.
He was annoyed at this abrupt exposure,
But speedily recovered his composure,
Deciding he must make the best of it;
And after they had chatted for a bit
A contract, with a large advance, was signed
(They had twelve monthly episodes in mind)
Giving them rights to his Sequestered State.
I hear the interest has been so great
That he will subdivide his thousand acres
To satisfy the clamouring forsakers
That yearn for toil to bring them inner peace,
And offer each a barren plot to lease –
He's absolutely stunned by what they'll pay
To throw up everything and get away.
So, having done his bit for Hand-to-Mouth,
He's looking for a mansion further south
Where he can sit at table as before,
And circulate the Sandeman's once more.

*   *100 Great Brits* (by this author too)
    Describes his life and philosophic view.

71

LORD ALI-BABA

Lord Ali-Baba was a Turk
Engaged in undercover work.
His life is wrapped in mystery,
But some suggest that it was he
Who aimed the pistol in his hand
At helpless Archduke Ferdinand,
Which started off the First World War.
And when, in 1934,
Hitler seized power, it was not
The future Führer's master-plot,
But Ali-Baba's – who was known
As One who stood behind the Throne,
Although this vital role of his
Was hidden from the histories.
A photograph of which I've heard
(Apparently a trifle blurred)
Reveals Ali-Baba's face
Not far from Harry Truman's place
At Potsdam, when he took the chair
With other Allied leaders there,
Discussing how to beat Japan;
For Ali-Baba was the man
Who made the President conclude
That Bombing would depress their mood.
In post-war London he resided,
And British policy was guided

By Ali-Baba, who, of course,
Amassed the Franco-British force
That Eden claimed *he* had despatched
When Nasser quite unfairly snatched
The Suez waterway. And then
When sands moved under No. 10
As Christine Keeler's winning ways
Made it unclear for several days
If Supermac could stay in power,
Our unsung Hero of the Hour
Went to Profumo in disguise,
Reproached him for his bare-faced lies
(He'd told the House he'd never met her)
And came back with the famous Letter
That got Macmillan off the hook!
His Life reads rather like a book,
And rumours even now persist
That he did not, in fact, exist.

LORD CALVIN

Lord Calvin thought the Bishops should not sit
On working groups that *re-wrote* Holy Writ.
The Bible sanctioned by the first King James
Sublimely justified its noble aims,
Giving the Word in words that thrilled the ears.
It had done so for some three hundred years!
How gross, to pander to the modern fashion
For so-called clarity instead of passion!
How can we *clarify* the Most Divine?
Is He revealed in the Written Line?
No, no! To seek him, tread the Lakeland hills –
Observe him in a clump of daffodils
Or in the sunrise breaking through the mist
(Lord Calvin was, you'll guess, a pantheist).
When a committee struggles to convey
What they suppose the Scribe had *meant* to say,
Out of the window goes the hallowed verse,
And we are left with gibberish – or worse!

Before this licensed meddling occurred,
John wrote 'In the beginning was the Word',
Which they improved to 'When all things began,
The Word already was.' Laugh if you can,
Howl if you must, at such a travesty;
But that's how John starts in the NEB
(*New English Bible*, 1961).
On reading this and other things they'd done,
Lord Calvin to his Library retired,
Drafted his Epitaph, and then expired.
'Dear Lord,' it ran, 'what I had hoped to do
Was come to Thee; now I must come to You.'

LORD CANTON

The reason that the present Lord Canton
Attracts attention (though he's getting on),
Is his concern that people's education
Lacks any formal training in Oration.
Since Electronics make a sigh a shout,
No wonder Voice Projection's dying out!
He's deafened an entire Albert Hall
Without the use of phonic aids at all;
And, getting quite excited on *Today,*
His volume blew the microphones away
And vaporised an all-important fuse
(Which meant a second reading of the News
While studio technicians tore their hair
Trying to get John Humphrys back on air).
The topic that ignited this explosion
Was what he called the Devilish Corrosion
Of ancient churches large and small alike

By loudspeakers, a console and a mike!
When thousands heard the Word of the Messiah,
Did He address them through an amplifier?
When churchgoing achieved its all-time peak,
With half the country going every week,
Why could the servants crammed in by the font
Hear so distinctly that they would not Want
In pastures green – in fact, they might be saved
Before those at the front, for whom they slaved?
The reason's very simple, he explained:
When they were studying to be ordained,
Those collared quartermasters of the Lord's
Were taught how to employ their *vocal cords.*
They'd throw their head back, lungs about to split
With God's good air, they'd gulped so much of it,
And blast the congregation with His thunder!
Now those pews gape; and is it any wonder,
When Modern Ministers prefer to squeak
Into a microphone, instead of Speak?
Perhaps, Lord Canton adds, deeply ironic,
They're not to blame for going Electronic,
Because the uproar of the modern day
Is so loud that it takes God's breath away!
He'll need a loudspeaker to be made out,
Until the Sigh once more becomes a Shout.

LORD FINCHLEY

Lord Finchley tried to mend the Electric Light,
But since he didn't do a screw up tight,
Two wires touched, the circuit overloaded,
And every light bulb in the house exploded.
The shock brought down the power lines that fed
The nearby towns of Tring and Berkhamsted,
Followed by even more dramatic scenes
When night's black cloak enveloped Milton Keynes.
Primeval terror gripped the stoutest heart
As pylons swayed and cables came apart
With flashes that lit up the sky, until
The land was dark from York to Selsey Bill.

★

Lord Finchley was completely unaware
That this derived from his unwise repair;
And having no alternative that night
To eating leftovers by candlelight
(And ending up with Peaches from a Tin),
His tolerance had worn extremely thin.

'It is our use of European Power
That preordained this Catastrophic Hour!
Let there be research (funded by the State)
So that our Sea-girt Isle may generate
A full sufficiency of Volts and Amps
To cook our food, and energise our lamps!'
He Chairs the influential Solar Panel,
And backs a plan to dam the English Channel,
Releasing tidal water twice a day.
Though much of Essex will be washed away,
It's up to everyone to Do Their Bit
To make sure that the Kingdom's lamps stay lit.

LORD HENRY CHASE

What happened to Lord Henry Chase?
Partaking in the Fastnet Race
(During the First Leg, outward bound),
He vanished and was never found!
The sea was calm, the pressure high,
No cloud besmirched the starry sky,
Nor was he sailing very fast –
The Peer, in fact, was coming last.
But when Forensic Experts boarded,
Their detailed report recorded
That near the stern, a rail was bent,
Which might have caused the accident,
If, half awake (or half asleep),
Lord Henry Chase fell in the deep
When, having tripped through lack of care,
His clutching hand grasped empty air.
Still, just before he went to sea
He'd taken out a Policy
To cover boating accidents
(Which showed his foresight and good sense),
The sum insured, should it be claimed,
Assigned to somebody unnamed
Who held a Lichtenstein account.
It was an adequate amount.
But then – guess what? A few years later,
A person south of the Equator
(Bolivia or some such place),

Who happened to recall his face,
Observed his Shade or Doppelgänger
Emerging from an aircraft hangar
Where it had parked its private plane;
The Thing was later seen again
Heading towards an English Bar
Near Plaza Mayor, Panama!
So ghosts exist, and walk about –
Lord Henry's leaves no room for doubt.

LORD HEYGATE

Lord Heygate had a troubled face
On hearing of a ruinous case
His furious neighbour was beginning,
And which he had no chance of winning.

★

Heygate had wanted to prevent
A rude solstitial event,
When guardians of the Ancient Laws
Would turn up in their 4x4s
And having donned Druidic gear
(Assuming that the sky was clear)
Blew horns to greet the rising Sun
And ravished Maidens one by one,
Who made a penetrating din.
Lord Heygate's patience wearing thin
(For every year the noise increased
As re-born Druids joined the feast),
He asked the host of these events,
Whose land lay just below his fence,
To find another sacred site
And let him have a quiet night.
This more than reasonable request
Received the answer: 'Be my guest –
I'll let you have a Sunrise Bride,
And stimulants will be supplied!'

The hint that he was thus inclined
Offended someone so refined,
So, on the eve, he went to bed,
A pillow covering his head,
Till uproar from the godless scene
Disturbed the Peer at two-fifteen.
Feeling excessively displeased,
He donned his dressing-gown, and seized
A spanner of enormous size
With which to give them a surprise.
The Founder of his noble pile
(A mansion in the Tudor style)
Had dammed a little stream, to make
A splendid ornamental lake,
Its waters held in by a sluice.
His spanner got the fixings loose,
And off the brimming water went,
Which terminated the event.

★

He realised he'd be strapped for cash
If judged to have been over-rash,
Which made it manifestly wise
To cut down and economise.
His superannuated Cook
Was given boots, and told to look
Among the puddles in the mud
From whence had flowed the fatal flood
For any Gudgeon, Tench, or Eel
On which to base his evening meal.

The servant did as he was bid,
And saw the corner of the lid
Of some colossal chest or trunk
That had, as it turned out, been sunk
In April 1644
When England bled in civil war.
The mud, which was extremely smelly,
Bequeathed the lord a Botticelli
(A work of unexampled power
Called *Aphrodite in the Shower*)
Which Heygate lifted out, revealing
The Cartoon for the Sistine Ceiling,
And other odds and ends as well,
Including works by Raphael,
And at the bottom, even better,
A file copy of a letter
Da Vinci sent to Mona Lisa,
Saying he hoped the Work would please her,
And what her husband had to pay
(Which still amuses her today).
These interesting finds of his,
When they come up at Sotheby's,
Will hardly leave him feeling short;
So he can settle, out of court,
Whatever sum they think is right
For getting washed away that night,
And give them, too, a small donation,
Which should secure an invitation
When they next celebrate the Sun.
It might, he says, be rather fun
(If he can join their Order too)
To do the things that Druids do.

LORD HIPPO

Lord Hippo suffered fearful loss
When he was made extremely cross
On finding an intruder thieving.
He asked the man if he'd mind leaving,
But all he did was turn his back
And keep on filling up his sack,
Which prompted, from the furious Peer,
Words I refrain from printing here.
The burglar, shocked beyond belief
At being called a Common Thief
(Since he was well up in the Law)
Asked Hippo what he took him for,
Explaining that until he'd left,
His sampling could not count as theft,
And therefore this insinuation
Might be the cause of Litigation.
Lord Hippo, grabbing back his wares,
Propelled the fellow down the stairs,
On which a besom had been laid
By Gladys Gubb, the parlour maid.
The Thief (or maybe I should say

The fellow who had called that day)
Tripped over the offending brush,
And in his cataclysmic rush
Hit Lady Hippo, who was standing
Arranging roses on the landing,
Which also hurt her quite a lot
And meant she'd need another pot.

★

The landmark trial of this Peer
Lasted the best part of a year,
Earning considerable fees.
The charges that he faced were these:
That (1) a reckless accusation
Had harmed the Plaintiff's reputation,
And (2) that due to gross neglect
A lucrative career was wrecked,
Since ruptured tendons in his knee
Had lessened his agility.
The Prosecution's case depended
On Gladys, who on oath contended
That while she swept the stairs, she heard
Lord Hippo use that fateful word.
In vain did the Defence declare

That (1) split a semantic hair,
And (2) was lost when he confessed
To having failed to warn his guest
That since the stairs were being swept
He should be careful where he stepped.
The damages (Ten Million Pounds)
Meant selling off the house and grounds
And starting up a B&B
At 14 Harbour Street, Torquay;
While Gladys told the waiting Press
She'd talk for 50 k, no less,
Starred in *EastEnders*, chatted, hosted,
And now her Life is being ghosted.

LORD LUCKY

Lord Lucky, by a curious fluke,
Escaped a well-deserved rebuke
For digging an enormous pit
And laying branches over it,
Plus grass and suchlike stuff he found
To make it seem like solid ground.
He was at Grandpa's, which was not
A very entertaining spot
In which to pass one's holidays
(He'd quickly sorted out the Maze,
Within whose geometric green
His second cousin, Gwendoline,
Refused to be induced to play,
Put off by his *naïveté*).
A rainy day became the cause
Of Lucky's project. Stuck indoors
He tried the Library, and found
A set of volumes, leather-bound,
With tales of a violent sort
In which resourceful white men fought
With natives, and beat off gorillas.
These eagerly awaited thrillers
(With frontispieces) were the rage
In Britain's high Victorian Age,
Although our more holistic sense
Dislikes their easy confidence.
But little Lucky, unaware

Of this impending moral snare,
Was quite enchanted, as he sat
With Stevenson, and Maryatt,
And Ballantyne, and other hands
That took him to exotic lands.
It was these authors' clear advice
On how to make a neat device
For catching Wild Beasts that made
Our hero set to with a spade.
A spot beyond the western wing
(By Vanbrugh) seemed promising,
For here his Grandpa liked to take
A short cut to the Upper Lake,
And, plunging through, would utter cries
Commensurate with his surprise.

★

But Fate had other plans in mind.
The weather, which remained unkind,
Kept Grandfather indoors, but seemed
Just right for villains who had schemed
To kidnap fetching Gwendoline.
Visualise the midnight scene!
The ladder to the second floor...
The maiden's unsuspecting snore...
The window raised without a sound...
The helpless figure gagged and bound –
Though in their hurry, they forgot
To double-check a vital knot,
And by the time she is outside

The captive has her legs untied!
Towards the Upper Lake she speeds
To find some cover in the reeds,
Her slender frame quite unaware
That at one point she's crossing air –
The trapping twigs that Lucky laid
Can easily support the maid!
Then cracking wood and bodies falling,
And shouts (the language is appalling),
Until the wretched men submit
And are extracted from the pit.
And then – how was the balance tilted!
In Lucky's arms his cousin wilted,
And they passed many blissful days
Seeking each other in the Maze...

They wed, and were with issue blessed,
And so eventually possessed
The house where it had all begun.
But Lucky (thinking of his son)
Exchanged those thrilling books he'd read
For prudent modern stuff instead.

LORD LUNDY

Lord Lundy from his earliest years
Stood out among his fellow peers
For being fussy about Food.
In infancy, this attitude
Made him reject whichever breast
In his considered view possessed
The merest smidgen of Caffeine,
Or Alcohol, or Tartrazine.
He soon revealed an innate sense
Of vitamins and nutrients,
And by the time he went to school
He understood the Kilojoule.

Soon afterwards, a moral voice
Began to influence his choice:
No fleshly protein would he take,
Inclining more to soya cake;
No orphaned egg would pass his lips,
Nor leather circumscribe his hips
Or shame his saddle, shoe or boot –
Though he would eat Contented Fruit
Picked kindly. In his later teens
This Peer was seized on by the Greens,
Earning a vigorous rebuke
From his Papa, the Fourteenth Duke,
Who thus addressed his son and heir:
'Your food-fads drive me to despair!
In my young days we simply ate
And drank, without a great debate
About how much of This and That...
P-o-l-y-u-n-s-a-t-u-r-a-t-e-d Fat?
The stuff had never been invented!
It's made you quite disoriented!
The shocking depths to which you've sunk!
I've never, ever, seen you drunk!'

★

The Greens were fighting an Election,
And their unanimous selection
Was Doris Thin, the Town Clerk's daughter,
Who lived on lettuces and water –
A lady who could not excite
Except by artificial light.

Her lost deposit (she came third)
From Lundy drew a tender word,
Together with a cheque he'd written
To cover costs: the two were smitten,
And by a candle's glancing rays
Sweetly indulged their salad days.
But oh! How transient would be
This chlorophyllic ecstasy!
A saboteur, who guessed the way
The Hunt would go on Boxing Day,
Jumped out and checked the leading horse:
The Fourteenth Duke's ballistic course
Projected him into a lake,
And our young hero had to take
His station in the House of Lords.
He walked beneath the serried swords
With Doris, in a state of fright
At what awaited him that night,
But Nature smiled, or so it seemed,
For very soon his Duchess teemed
And was delivered of a Son,
Who was informed by everyone:
'Oh, what a pretty boy you are –
The image of your Grandpapa!'
He was: for he'd soon had enough
Of the anaemic fat-free stuff
His mother oozed, and made it clear
He'd much prefer a Mug of Beer,
On which the growing fellow thrived;
And once his little teeth arrived
He'd tuck into a steak, done rare,

And then a runny Camembert
Washed down with Châteauneuf-du-Pape
To help him settle for his nap.

★

His parents, I need hardly say,
Viewed his reversion with dismay;
But after counselling, they saw
That Nature, red in tooth and claw,
Gives every Beast an appetite
For what is naturally right,
And that it does not do to think
Too much about our food and drink.
So Doris lost (as you may guess)
Her former lack of shapeliness,
And Lundy filled the cellar space
With port and claret by the case,
And bought bits of the Côte de Nuits
To keep them all in Burgundy.

LORD ROEHAMPTON

During a late election Lord
Roehampton vanished overboard,
And was reported Lost at Sea.
A would-be Liberal MP
(A lady he had taken to
Despite their differences in view)
Urged him to roam the Solent waters
And try to canvass more supporters.
He buzzed round with an outboard motor,
Exhorting every floating voter
To choose her, when they made their mark;
But with the evening getting dark
He headed landwards, and, it's thought,
Took red for starboard, green for port,
Which meant he faced a ferry's bows
And not its stern, when nearing Cowes.
At least this meant he never learned
His friend was not the one returned.

LORD UNCLE TOM

Lord Uncle Tom was different from
Most Uncles I have seen.
For they were black or white or pink,
But Uncle Tom was *Green!*

    He ran his house on energy
    That Nature could renew.
    He harnessed Sun, he harnessed Wind –
    He harnessed Horses too!

        A simple notice you would see
        Beside his parkland gate.
        No fossil-fuelled transport here.
        Please ring the bell and wait.

The sound of hooves would greet the ear...
Into the gig you'd get
(He might send something with a hood
If it was really wet).

    No snarl of chainsaws in the woods
    Where yellow-hatted men
    Held engines that did all the work!
    On his land, once again,

Tree met the axe on equal terms.
And when the deed was done,
It kissed the earth with dignity –
The battle lost and won.

Propellers set upon his roof
Rotated in the breeze
And churned out electricity.
But not content with these,

He turned vast mirrors to the Sun,
Condensed its seething rays,
And heated tanks of water up
(Except on cloudy days).

But when the sunshine got too hot
The boiler boiled dry,
And set his Stately Home ablaze
Beneath the summer sky.

Lord Uncle Tom is not as Green
As in those days of yore.
He's grabbing blocks of BP shares,
And drives a 4x4.

Note
Don't mess about with Nature's forces.
If you'd be Greener, stick to horses.

THE AUTHOR

There is a literary man
Who, feeling underpaid,
Demanded more – and so began
A personal crusade.

He told his Publisher: 'Now look –
It's most unfair to me.
Readers pay £10 for my book,
And I get 30p!'

'Your business logic is naïve,'
Came back the stern rebuff.
'Rejoice in what you *do* receive –
We think it's quite enough!

'Our profits daily drain away;
We're in the Dealers' grip.
Stop grumbling about your pay
And stick to Authorship!'

He sought a Dealer, who replied:
'We're *saving* them expense!
We handle all the wholesale side –
That's basic business sense!

'What? *Screwing* them? We're screwed ourselves!
In fact we're in a vice!
To get stock on the High Street shelves
We've got to take *their* price!'

'Calm down!' the bookshop's buyer said.
'Stop making such a fuss!
Your work would not be seen and read
If it were not for us!

'*Hand over fist?* Look by the door!
We're selling 3 for 2!
If we cut margins any more,
We shan't be stocking you!

'Your Publisher's the one to blame.
Demand a bigger share!
You have? Oh well, they're all the same.
You're right – it's most unfair!'

The Author, having done the rounds,
Can now more clearly see
Why, from a book that costs £10,
He gets just 30p.

Note
The firm whose payment prompted this remorse
Is not the present Publisher, of course.

THE EXAMPLE

John Henderson, an unbeliever,
 Was in the hands of the Receiver
  After a careful audit showed
   He owned far less than what he owed.
    His business having come to grief,
     He found a measure of relief
      In Matthew 9:24,
       Which says the poor will profit more
        Than richer folk, when they complete
         Their spiritual balance sheet
          (A doctrine that is tailor-made
           For those unfortunate in trade).
            John's creditors, once they had found
             They'd get just 10p in the pound,
              Besieged his Hampstead maisonette.
               He cried: 'Good friends, I'm in your debt –
                A debt I cannot hope to pay!
                 Thank you for showing me the way
                  To true wealth, which I'd almost missed!
                   I'll quote from the Evangelist!'
                    The mob, legitimately vexed,
                     Paid no heed to the Sacred Text,
                      And even as the Bankrupt spoke
                       He disappeared in clouds of smoke,
                        For they'd begun a conflagration
                         By way of venting their frustration.
                          Since his domain was his no more,

Now being forfeit to the Law,
He didn't mind the blaze at all;
In fact, its loss enhanced his call
To seek a new Redemptive Creed –
The ashes of financial greed
Confirming his Imperative
That wealth is judged by what you give.
He works from premises he's leased
(Five minutes' walk from Aldgate East)
Where clients plead with him to take
Out of the megabucks they make
Whatever share (or one-off sum)
Will guarantee Elysium.
It's up to him, of course, to see
That it is spent on Charity,
And could there be a better cause
Than his, which promulgates God's Laws?
This means that he has grown more wealthy
Than Matthew would consider healthy,
But though the needle's eye is small,
John risks it for the Good of All.

WILLIAM SHAND

There was a man called William Shand,
Who bought a Castle (second-hand)
And asked some friends, if they were free,
To come and live communally.
A TV company would share
The cost of salvage and repair
If they might turn up now and then
With microphones and cameramen
To film as things got into shape
And store their highs and lows on tape,
To be transmitted week by week
With evening viewing at its peak.
To forestall chances of dissent
At moments of discouragement,
He chose those people he knew well
From having shared a prison cell,
When they'd pass happy hours away
Conceiving schemes where crime would pay.
The ones who liked to work outside
Were in the charge of Hugh MacBride
(A Scot), whose methods were renowned
For bearing fruit in stubborn ground –
His partner and prodigious brood
Washed up and cooked and served the food.
A dealer in the things they'd need
Got favourable rates indeed
By paying cash and therefore waiving

The paperwork, which meant a saving;
Their bookkeeper (and Bookie) saw
That they were making rather more
Than could be guessed from the accounts
(Spirits in copious amounts
Soon occupied the cellar space,
Of which the Excise had no trace);
And lastly, but by no means least,
Came Algernon, a defrocked Priest,
Who graced their meals, soothed their cares,
And led them all in evening prayers.

★

But William's optimistic scheme
Was destined to remain a dream
Because (he'll ruefully admit)
He'd made too good a job of it!
The fellowship, as he had meant,
Worked perfectly, without dissent.
All did their bit, all shared the load;
The roof was fixed, the land was sowed;
Each week they held a Moot, reviewing
The various jobs that needed doing,
Without a voice in protest raised;
And in the chapel, God was praised.
The programme makers were aghast –
They'd banked on strife; but weeks had passed
Without an angry word at all!
The ratings soon began to fall,
Since people happy with their lot

Have no place in the peak-time slot,
And it was shifted very soon
To 3.10 in the afternoon.
The plug was pulled, the funding ended,
All operations were suspended,
And William's started to prepare
Another Castle in the Air.

PART 4

A MODERN ALPHABET

Consisting of Neologisms and words that have acquired new significance since Grandparents were young.

A is for ADDITIVE

If you notice an E
Such as E123
On the food you select –
As you will, I expect,
If it's Ready-to-Eat
(Once subjected to heat) –
Then you ought to beware,
For an Additive's there.
If you think you might try
A Microwave Pie
The next time you're shopping,
It's worthwhile stopping
To look at the back
Of the colourful pack.
Then pause for a minute,
Consider what's in it,
Put it back on the shelf,
And bake one yourself.

B is for **BIODEGRADABLE**

AN EPITAPH

After my Soul has flown away
Do this last thing for me...
Allow my Substance to decay
Biodegradably.

It is a mouthful, I admit,
Like many modern terms.
But if you want the gist of it,
Let Me be Food for Worms!

C is for **CARBON DIOXIDE**

It isn't yet clear what we're going to do
About carbon dioxide (i.e., CO_2).
We're producing vast volumes when oil is burned
(Or coal for that matter); and now we have learned
That it holds in the heat when the Sun warms the ground,
And Meteorologists claim to have found
That the average temperature's steadily rising
Thanks to carbon dioxide – which isn't surprising
When you think how the world population's increasing,
And the rise in consumption is therefore unceasing.
But can we cut down and conserve our supplies
When the World's run by Business, whose profits *must* rise?
Can Tides and the Wind take the measure of coal?
Is Carbonless Thrift an achievable goal?
Will things get still worse as our children grow older?
Go by Bus, not by Car – help to make the World Colder!

D is for DVD

You never see me work, but work I do.

My real name is much too long for you.

I'm all the rage right now, but just you wait –

Ten years at most, and I'll be out of date.

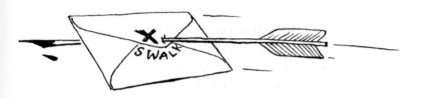

E is for EMAIL

Dear friend,
   By electronic might,
   And almost at the speed of light,
   This message flashes on your screen,
   No sooner signed and sent than seen
   (Though if it's not addressed with care,
   It could go almost anywhere).
   Oh, what a loss we have sustained
   Since Writing Desk and Inkwell reigned!
   The passionate flood that swept the sheet,
   Kissed by the blotter, once complete;
   The folded creases gently pressed,
   The matching envelope addressed
   To that sweet Bower of Delight;
   And, having got the post code right,
   You gave the flap a luscious lick
   (Though some you simply pressed to stick),
   And lastly – sweet delay indeed –
   You could not find the stamp you'd need!
   Some money rattled from a drawer;
   Umbrella, coat, a slamming door,

And through the whirling flakes you'd dart,
The letter snug beside your heart,
Till, having battled all that way,
A sign says *Early Closing Day*...
And then, once posted through the slot,
How thrilling your diurnal lot!
The wakeful night, the morning's wait,
The clicking of the garden gate,
The heavy tread, the rat-tat-tat,
The muddled missives on the mat
Through which, on bended knee, you sift...
The free champagne, the tempting gift,
But that for which you'd give your All
Alone there in the chilly hall,
You do not find. There is no letter...
Some say that email is *better!*
I write to you, you answer me
An hour later, prefixed 'Re',
And all at negligible cost.
That's true – but think of what we've lost!

F is for
FRIENDS REUNITED

'Hallo? You got my email? *Fine!*
No – ladies first! The floor is mine?
All right then! Where shall I begin?
My prowess with the violin?
The *Orchestra!* The row we made!
What was the instrument you played?
The *Glockenspiel?* I forgot!
Well yes, I still play quite a lot.
Oh, the odd Prom... What about you?
Are you still keen on music too?
You've given up the Glockenspiel?
It's lost its earlier appeal?
That *is* a shame! Now let me hear
What *you've* done! Followed a career?
A Law Lord? Really? Well I never!
I'd no idea you were so clever!
I really fancied you, back then!
And how old were you? Pushing ten?
I thought of you the other day –
You took me down that alleyway
And let me pull your knickers down.
You charged the others half a crown –
At least I think that's what they said.
Hallo? Oh blast! The line's gone dead!'

G is for GREEN

Before Green issues bothered us,
A person of this hue
Was either very envious
Or just about to Spew.
This quirk of etymology
Might make some people think
How much more pleasing it would be
If Chlorophyll were Pink.

H is for HOLISTIC

If one takes the Holistic view
(The Green philosophy),
It means that everything *you* do
Has some effect on *me*.

> The whole is more than just its parts,
> Or so Holism states.
> And that is where the trouble starts –
> For *everything relates*.

A spinney's more than just its trees –
It's habitats galore;
It binds the earth, it blocks the breeze,
It gives us wood to saw...

> And when the fuel in the jet
> That speeds you to the Sun
> Helps make our planet warmer yet,
> Reflect on what you've done...

Our balance could begin to tip
If Gaia is displeased.
A mountainside can start to slip
Because a skier sneezed...

> But still, however hard I try,
> I'm rather doubtful whether
> The flutter of a butterfly
> Upset last summer's weather!

I is for ICONIC

To saintly icons, lights are lit
And knees are often bowed;
But now the term is stretched a bit,
And of this motley crowd
Not all are Saints in how they live,
So get their morals checked,
Or find another adjective
To signal your respect.

J is for JOGGING

J is for Jogging, in tracksuit and trainers,
A pursuit much approved of by Healthy Campaigners.
It tones up your muscles, is good for your heart,
And gives every morning an excellent start
If you puff along pavements for up to an hour
And tuck into muesli while having a shower.
But remember Ted Wragg, whose rebellious views
About State Education made national news...
I'd see him out jogging (although he'd retired),
Till on his last run he collapsed and expired.
We were shocked when we heard what had happened to Ted –
So by all means go jogging, but don't end up Dead.

K is for **KILOMETRE**

The Kilometre I deplore.
Its logic makes no sense.
Our Footsteps ought to matter more
Than our Circumference!

Yes! Metrication's based upon
The distance round the Earth!
Pounds, gallons, furlongs – all have gone,
Thanks to our planet's girth!

We should have voted with our Feet
And said 'To hell with metres!'
But even though we're in retreat,
We still drink Pints, not litres!

L is for LAWYERS

My L is for Lawyers, who like Litigation,
And unceasingly urge us to seek Compensation.
I don't intend spending more time on them here;
If you want an example, please turn to 'Maria'.

M is for MOBILE

No Modern Child is allowed
To wander lonely as a cloud.

N is for
NEIGHBOURHOOD WATCH

The older generation sighs:
'What is our country coming to?
The Law and Order that we knew
Is vanishing before our eyes!

'Young people grew up with respect!
They didn't burgle or assault!
It's their neglectful parents' fault!
They simply wander round unchecked!'

But is this reason really true?
Does it come down to civic sense?
Or do we have more incidents
Because we've fewer Men in Blue?

Till roughly fifty years ago
We had a Village Copper here.
And so the Law was always near,
To tell the time and say 'What-ho!'

As long as he was on the spot
The vandals were as good as gold.
But he is gone, his house is sold,
And now the Watch is all we've got.

By one criterion, it's true,
The change has been a great success.
That black and yellow sign costs less
Than paying for a Man in Blue!

O is for OZONE

O_3 stands for Ozone, intangible stuff.

Of its cousin O_2 we've got more than enough

(O_2 stands for oxygen, as you're aware,

But O_3 is a layer high up in the air).

Well, back in the Sixties we started to spray

Hair, food, flies and windscreens – which made it decay,

For the aerosols loosed with each whoosh from a can

Turned O_3 to O_2, and this led to a ban,

Since Ozone makes harmless the rays of the Sun –

Without its effect, life might not have begun!

Our whooshing and squirting have blown a huge hole

Beyond the Antipodes, over the Pole,

And Aussies don't go out, unless they have packed a

Sun-filtering cream of formidable factor.

But modern propellants released by the trigger

Should mean that the Hole won't go on getting bigger,

And O_2 (so we hope) will turn back to O_3.

Which leaves us that problem beginning with C...

P is for PIN

The Cashless Revolution's under way!
In twenty years from now, all sums you pay
    Will be by PIN, however great or small,
    For notes and coins will not be seen at all!
Whether you buy a house, divorce or yacht
(Or something else that comes to quite a lot),
    Or make your contribution in a pew,
    Tapping your code is all you'll have to do!
Tramps, buskers, gypsies, all will be cash-free
When we at last abolish currency,
    Nor will Salvation's Soldiers shake their tin –
    You'll swipe your card for them, and punch your PIN!
Although this concept may seem rather strange,
Think of the gains – no fumbling for change,
    No queues at cash machines, no visored man
    Emerging from inside an Armoured Van;
And since the risk of raids will disappear,
There'll be no need to glass-in the cashier
    (Though with no cash, it's logical to ask
    What function would be served by such a task).
We shall escape the tyranny of Gold;
And if Great Britain's bought more than she's sold,
    One keystroke will make up the sales we lack,
    And two may even put us in the black!
So get a PIN right now – you won't regret it,
Until your mind goes blank, and you forget it.

Q is for **THE QUEEN** and **QUEUING**

We used to stand to hear The Queen
When entertained by stage or screen.
That's something we no longer do –
But, come what may, we love to Queue.

R is for **RELIGIOUS BELIEF**

It's not at all odd
That Believing in God
Is harder the more that we know.

If science makes plain
What we couldn't explain,
Then what can we possibly owe

To an ultimate cause,
If our physical laws
Make it clear why the World is just so?

But with no Divine Plan
That resulted in Man,
We've delivered a serious blow

To the thought that Up There
(Although goodness knows where)
There's a Heaven to which we shall go.

Still, which might be worse?
For our Souls to disperse
(If upon our decease they're *de trop*)?

Or to meet those we love
In a new place Above –
Plus a lot we'd prefer left Below?

S is for SUSTAINABILITY

This buzzword delivers much less than it should,
And I'll use the example of pulp made from wood.
If you're worried that novels are bad for our trees,
You may gain reassurance from words such as these
(Below the small print on Conditions of Trade):
Our policy is to use Paper that's made
From Wood grown in Forests that could be Sustained.
And the way that they're managed (it's also explained)
Conforms to the Country's Conditions for Felling.
If you ponder this boast, it is hardly compelling!
A forest's sustained only *IF* it's replanted;
The terms upon which any licence is granted
Are up to the government; and, as we've seen,
By no means all countries are equally Green.
But don't be distraught if you can't guarantee
That your novel was grown on a well-managed tree;
The goodness it's used can be fully replaced
If you shred it at once for Compostible Waste.

T is for **TRANSPARENCY**

We once took the view
That if you *saw through*
        A scheme or suggestion
        It was open to question
If you ought to pursue it.
If you *couldn't* see through it
        (At least at first sight)
        Then it might be all right.
But it's now a mistake
To make something opaque,
        So suspicious are we
        Of what we can't see!
Which makes me conclude
That however we're viewed
        (If we're seen through or not)
        We're a Devious Lot.

U is for U-TURN

Such loss of face cannot embarrass you.
U-turns are things that other Parties do.

V is for VOLUNTEER

My V is for the Modern Volunteer –
The person Belloc also thought of here
(Though his patrolled the Empire's defences).
For tea and cake and travelling expenses,
This selfless army, variously skilled,
Help fellow citizens and feel fulfilled.
They lend an ear to someone's urgent plea
When they are desperate; or out at sea
They pluck a victim from the ocean's jaws;
Or they explain the local planning laws
To someone keen to build a new extension;
Nor can I possibly omit to mention
The lady in the hospital, who'll say:
'Please follow me. Not quite so cold today!'
To want to be of use, to Do Your Bit,
And not to make a penny out of it,
Is not quite such an altruistic act
As blowing up a market when it's packed
And paying with your life; but even so,
We should not rate our Volunteers too low.

W is for WASTE

We fill another Albert Hall
(In volume) every day,
Thanks to the cheerful men who call
And take our bags away.

> We cannot win this wasteful war,
> But we'd have more success
> If we Made Do and Mended more,
> And Packaged rather less.

X is for X

X is the mark that you make when you choose
The MP you hope will accord with your views,
Or (more likely) the Party your leaning supports.
You stand all alone with your last-minute thoughts
In the rickety cubicle fetched from a store,
Where people have pondered this question before,
And it's right to reflect for a moment or two
On the power that others have given to you
To make a small X with the pen on its chain
That votes governments out, or returns them again.
Alone with your conscience, where no one can know
Against which of the names your endorsement will go,
You forget all the fuss about fiddled accounts
And donations exceeding permitted amounts,
And the half-truths, the sound bites, the organised leaks,
The conviction that no one in government speaks
What they really believe, in their keenness to please
(And S stands for Spinning as well as for Sleaze!);
And you stamp on the thought that the name you've selected
(If others agree, and your person's elected)
May not be the agent of change you desire,

Despite what it said in the colourful flyer.
Just be grateful for being entitled by law
To stand in the cubicle fetched from the store,
And make a small X with the pen on its chain –
A right which your forebears demanded in vain,
And got gaoled or killed for proclaiming their case.
So give them a thought in your moment of grace!
But why fuss about X, since it's not at all new,
And my Alphabet's meant to list modern words? True!
But there's bound to be change, and the paper and pen
And the cubicle won't be required again;
You'll just sit at your laptop, select an MP,
And signal approval by pressing a key.
So this is a function of X that we'll miss,
Though it's likely, I think, to remain as a Kiss.

Y is for YOB

This Uncouth Youth (that's what *Yob* means)
Besmirches our good name.
Is he a product of his genes,
Or is his Home to blame?

> Is our potential fixed from birth?
> Are we born High or Low?
> Does everyone have innate worth?
> We thought so, long ago...

Or, were he talked to as a child,
And given things to do,
Would he be less perverse and wild?
(That is the Modern View.)

> But whether it's Environment,
> Or Yobs are Yobs from birth,
> There is a widespread sentiment
> That all have equal worth.

So give the Yob a cheerful grin
And hug him when you should.
For though he'd like to do you in,
In God's eyes he is good.

Z is for ZERO

Z is for Zero, which not long ago

Was referred to in speaking as 'Nought' or as 'O',

Until numerate people began to insist

That this was an error we ought to resist,

For 'O' is a letter, and 'Nought' stands for 'Nil'

(Though I have to admit I use both of them still).

But as for the Digits, I do not intend

To rhyme them as well, for my Zero's my End!

ENVOI

THE ELECTRON

An apocalyptic glimpse that Mr Belloc might have enjoyed

Electrons, in their native state,
Whizz round at a tremendous rate,
And as they whirl, they jump and spin
According to the mood they're in.
It never ceases to amaze
That stuff so random in its ways
Can, at the pressing of a key,
Compute with seeming certainty.
These wanton fellows' antics make
Arithmetic a piece of cake,
Keep tabs on what a shop is selling,
Trap speeding cars and check our spelling,
Tell navigators where they're going,
And how much overdraft you're owing,
Without a single careless slip,
When sprinkled on a Microchip
(Though all their efforts lumped together
Could not foretell the English weather).
But is it really due to Chance,
Or does God orchestrate their dance?
If so, suppose one day He thought
He'd spin a One into a Nought...

★

Oh, then would Chaos have its fling,
And Misrule govern everything!
When 2 + 2 makes only 3,
What hope for High Technology?
Your clever car is up the spout;
Your keypad locks you in (or out);
Planes change direction in mid-flight;
A weather forecast turns out right,
And timekeepers run fast or slow
And finally refuse to go.
Then will the need to tell the hour
Turn faces upwards to the tower
Deep-founded in the earthly dust,
Where Sinners mingle with the Just,
So adding 2 and 2, you see,
Is risking much Uncertainty.
Forget electrons, *think* instead –
And try to do it in your head.

100 GREAT BRITS

A rhyming history
from Bede to Beckham

James Muirden

100 GREAT BRITS

A Rhyming History from Bede to Beckham

James Muirden

ISBN: 978 84024 611 7   Hardback   £9.99

'James Muirden's is a marvellous art:
Presenting complex thoughts in rhyme
Until they're tattooed on your heart
And this book's a winner, every time!'

Ian McMillan, poet and author

'*Characters from all walks of British history, from Alfred the Great to Christopher Wren, are summed up in these mini-biographies in amusing verse. Rhymes are easily remembered and offer a fresh way of learning new facts about our most famous citizens*'

THE GOOD BOOK GUIDE

www.summersdale.com